🐝 little bee books

A division of Bonnier Publishing
853 Broadway, New York, New York 10003
Copyright © 2016 by Bonnier Publishing
All rights reserved, including the right of reproduction in whole or in part in any form.
LITTLE BEE BOOKS is a trademark of Bonnier Publishing Group, and associated colophon is a trademark of Bonnier Publishing Group.
Manufactured in the United States   LB 0216
First Edition 10 9 8 7 6 5 4 3 2 1

Library of Congress Cataloging-in-Publication Data:
Names: Ohlin, Nancy, author. | Larkum, Adam, illustrator.
Title: Blast back! : ancient Egypt / by Nancy Ohlin ; illustrated by Adam Larkum.
Description: First edition. | New York : little bee books, 2016. |
Includes bibliographical references.
Subjects: LCSH: Egypt—Civilization—To 332 B.C.—Juvenile literature. |
Egypt--History—To 332 B.C.—Juvenile literature.
Classification: LCC DT61 .O36 2016 | DDC 932.01--dc23
LC record available at http://lccn.loc.gov/2015039047

Identifiers: LCCN 2015039047|
ISBN 9781499801163 (pbk) | ISBN 9781499801170 (hc) | ISBN 9781499804034 (eBook)

littlebeebooks.com
bonnierpublishing.com

BLAST BACK!

ANCIENT EGYPT

by Nancy Ohlin   illustrated by Adam Larkum

little bee books

CONTENTS

AFRICA

MEDITERRANEAN SEA

ANCIENT EGYPT

NILE

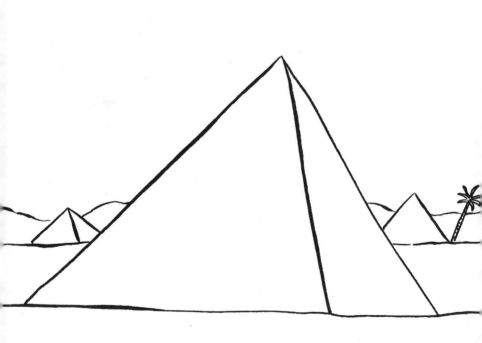

INTRODUCTION

When you hear people talk about "Ancient Egypt," you might think of things like mummies and pyramids. But what was Ancient Egypt *really* like? What did people do for fun? What kinds of pets did they have? And what were those pyramids for, anyway?

Let's blast back in time for a little adventure and find out. . . .

A BRIEF HISTORY OF ANCIENT EGYPT

You're wondering: What exactly is Ancient Egypt?

Ancient Egypt is a civilization. "Civilization" means the society, culture, and way of life of a particular time and place.

It's "ancient" because it's more than five thousand years old.

Ancient Egypt would not have been possible without the Nile River and rain. Lots of rain. Every summer, heavy rains to the south of Egypt made the water level of the river rise. The river flooded and soaked the lands along its banks.

This watery, goopy mud became rich, fertile soil that was perfect for farming. People moved to this area and began growing wheat, barley, flax, and other crops. They formed villages. Eventually, they split into two districts: Upper Egypt and Lower Egypt, also known as the "Two Lands."

Around five thousand years ago, the Two Lands united and became the kingdom of Egypt. This event is often considered to be the beginning of Ancient Egypt. The civilization lasted for

Ancient Egypt can be divided roughly into these key periods:

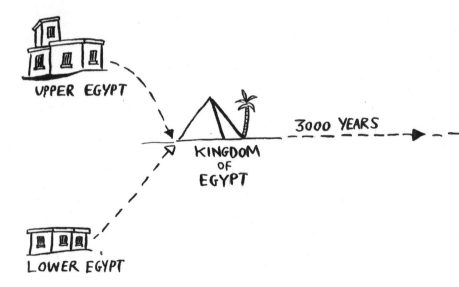

UPPER EGYPT

3000 YEARS

KINGDOM OF EGYPT

LOWER EGYPT

approximately three thousand years, until Egypt was folded into the Roman Empire (and possibly even later, until the Islamic conquest of Egypt). The country of Egypt still exists today, although it is no longer called a "kingdom."

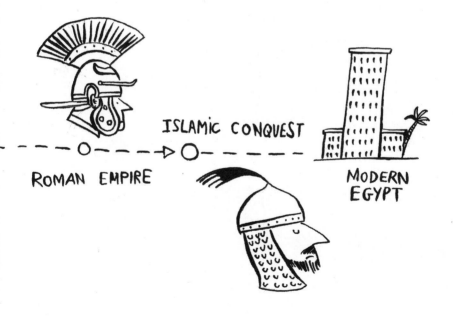

ISLAMIC CONQUEST

ROMAN EMPIRE

MODERN EGYPT

UPPER EGYPT

LOWER EGYPT

3000 YEARS

Experts are still trying to figure out dates, names, and other details regarding Ancient Egypt. It was a long time ago, and we don't have all the necessary records and remains to be absolutely certain about everything. New discoveries and new theories continue to be made. Egyptology, the study of Ancient Egypt, is a fascinating field!

ROMAN EMPIRE

ISLAMIC CONQUEST

MODERN EGYPT

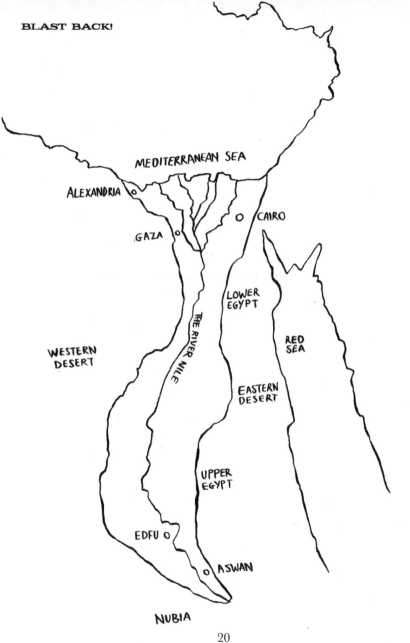

GEOGRAPHY AND CLIMATE

If you could see Egypt as it was thousands of years ago, you would notice a lot of interesting things.

Like today's Egypt, Ancient Egypt was in northeastern Africa on the banks of the Nile River. Even back then, the Nile was the longest river in the world. And even back then, it was home to animals like crocodiles and hippos.

There were farms, towns, and villages up and down the river on both sides. Beyond them was desert—miles and miles of desert. Some nomads lived in the desert.

Many houses were set on raised ground near the river and some may have been close to the edge of the desert, too. This was because the Ancient Egyptians wanted to prevent their homes from washing away during floods. (This doesn't happen anymore, thanks to a big dam that was constructed in the 1960s called the Aswan High Dam.)

The houses were built out of mud bricks, which worked well in the arid, or dry, climate. If it had rained a lot in Egypt, the mud bricks might have dissolved and turned into plain old mud!

The climate of Egypt has become even more arid over time. Weather-wise, there are two seasons: a hot summer, which goes from May to October, and a mild winter, which goes from November to April.

Farmer's Calendar

In Ancient Egypt, farmers split the year into three seasons. Each season corresponded with what was happening with the Nile River:

Akhet (June to September): The flooding season. Farmers couldn't farm during this time. This season was also referred to as "the inundation."

Peret (October to February): The growing season.

Shomu (March to May): The harvesting season.

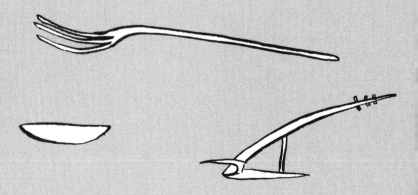

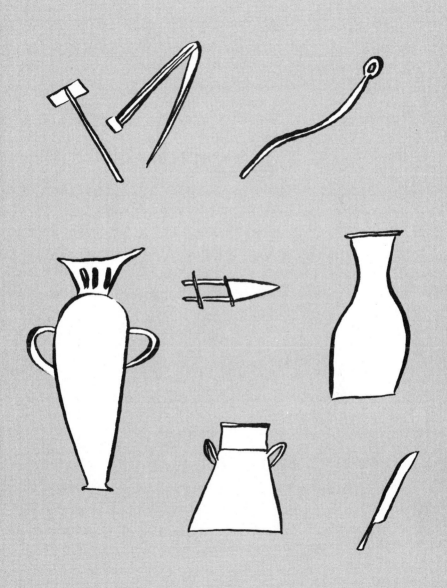

27

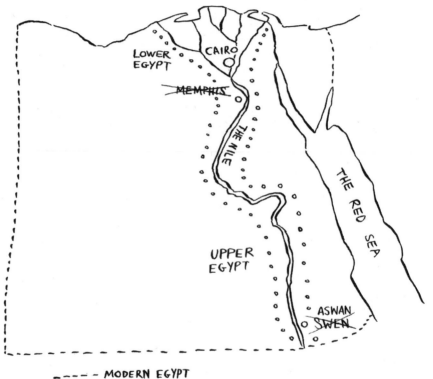

The geography of Egypt has also changed. When you look at a map of Ancient Egypt, you'll notice it's a little different from a map of present-day Egypt. Both Egypts are bordered by the Mediterranean Sea to the north, the Red Sea to the east, Libya to the west, and Sudan to the south. But Ancient Egypt has some cities that don't appear in present-day Egypt, like Memphis. And present-day Egypt has some cities that don't appear in Ancient Egypt, like Cairo. Some cities are the same but have changed names, like Aswan, which was known as Swen in Ancient Egypt.

GETTING AROUND

There were many great places to visit in Ancient Egypt, like pyramids and temples. But how would people get to them? The Ancient Egyptians didn't have planes, trains, or automobiles. There were very few roads, and most of them were unpaved and dusty.

That's where the Nile River comes in.

The Ancient Egyptians used their river as a kind of water highway, and boats were like their water cars. People could take short or long trips on boats. Fishermen could fish from them. Boats could also be used to carry cargo such as grain, cattle, or granite stone for building.

The earliest boats were constructed out of reeds from the papyrus plant. Back then, papyrus reeds were cheaper and easier to come by than wood. Papyrus boats worked well for short trips and fishing. Oars and poles were used to steer. (The word "papyrus" refers not just to the plant but also to a paper-like material made from the plant.)

Eventually, the Ancient Egyptians began constructing boats out of wood, which was stronger and longer lasting than papyrus. Cedar trees from Lebanon were a favorite building material. Rafts, barges, ferries, and war ships were made of wood; so were state ships for transporting kings and other important people.

Cargo ships were necessary for trading supplies with other countries. Many of the wooden boats had a sail in the middle that would catch the wind and push the boat down the Nile.

Besides traveling by boat, people walked a lot to get around. They also used donkeys for riding and hauling heavy loads. There were no camels or horses, which came later in Egypt's history. And vehicles with wheels, like wagons and chariots,

didn't exist yet either. People did use sledges and litters. Sledges looked like big wooden sleds and were pulled along by people or animals. Litters were carrying chairs or beds that sat on poles.

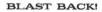

Up and Down the Nile River

The Nile River flows from south to north. When you sail down the Nile, you're sailing north toward the Mediterranean Sea. When you sail up the Nile, you're sailing south away from the Mediterranean Sea. That's because the term "downriver" means to go toward the mouth of a river, or where it empties out, and the mouth of the Nile River is the Mediterranean Sea. "Upriver" means to go toward the source of a river, or where it starts; the Nile has several sources south of the equator.

Remember Upper Egypt and Lower Egypt? Upper Egypt is called that because it's near the upper, or southern, part of the Nile. Lower Egypt is near the lower, or northern, part of the Nile.

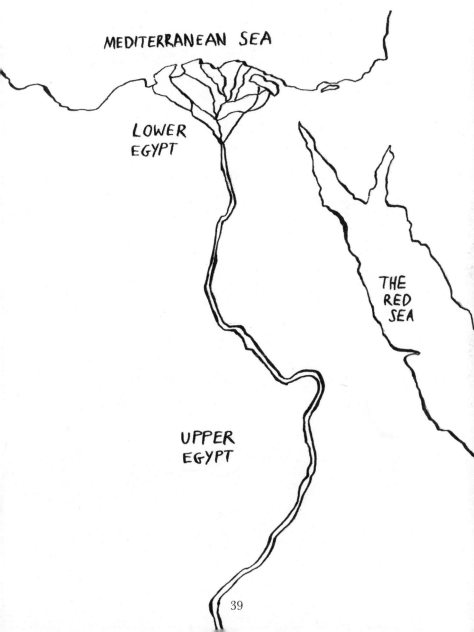

MEDITERRANEAN SEA

LOWER
EGYPT

THE
RED
SEA

UPPER
EGYPT

39

GODS AND GODDESSES

Many temples lined the Nile River. Inside the temples, a priest might be found polishing a statue of a bird, and even putting perfume, makeup, and clothes on the bird.

Confused?

Well, that bird wasn't just any bird—it was the god Horus!

Back then, Egyptians believed that gods and goddesses, or deities, ruled the world. At one point, they believed that these deities came from one original deity, the sun god Re. According to one myth, Re created himself out of a sea of chaos and then continued creating more gods.

After this, more and more deities were born. Some were good deities. Some were bad deities. Many of them had a specific job to do, like curing diseases or making sure the seasons changed.

Like Horus, some of them were represented by animals. Nekhbet, the goddess of Upper Egypt, was represented by a vulture. Tawaret, the protector of pregnancy and childbirth, was represented by a creature that was part hippo, part lion, and part crocodile.

A temple was considered to be the home of a god or goddess, and a statue inside the temple was considered his or her earthly form. It was the job of the priest to take care of the statue by washing it, dressing it, offering food to it, and also carrying it outside for festivals.

Obelisks stood in front of many of the temples, in pairs. An obelisk is a tall, four-sided pillar that is shaped like a pyramid at the top. Some obelisks were likely built to worship the sun god Re. They were usually decorated with hieroglyphs that honored Re as well as the kings who commissioned the obelisks.

Important Egyptian Gods and Goddesses

Osiris was the god of the underworld and fertility. He was one of the most important deities in Ancient Egypt.

Horus was the god of the sky and Osiris's son. It was believed that when a king died, he became Osiris, and his living son, the new king, became Horus.

Isis was the wife of Osiris and mother of Horus.

Seth was the god of the sky and thunderstorms. He was also the brother of Osiris and is said to have murdered him.

Anubis was the god of the dead.

Apophis was the god of chaos.

Sekhmet was the goddess of war.

Bastet was the goddess of cats
(and one of Re's daughters).

Hathor was the goddess of love, fertility, the sky, and women.

Thoth was the god of the moon, writing, and learning.

Wadjet was the goddess of Lower Egypt.

PHARAOHS

According to the Ancient Egyptians, the sun god Re didn't just create gods and goddesses. He also created the kings of Egypt, who were known as pharaohs.

The word pharaoh means "great estate." It originally referred to the palaces that the kings of Egypt lived in. Later, the kings themselves were called pharaohs. Ancient Egyptians thought of their pharaohs as part god and part human.

The pharaoh was very powerful—the most powerful person in all of Egypt. He was referred to as the "Lord of the Two Lands." He was also known as the "High Priest of Every Temple." It was his job to keep the gods and goddesses happy so his kingdom would have order, harmony, truth, and justice, or *maat*. He built temples. He performed rituals. He was in charge of Egypt's government and army. He made laws and enforced them.

The pharaoh was also very rich. He was the owner of everything and everyone in Egypt. He lived in several palaces with his family and servants. He was likely married to a queen, although he might have had a harem of extra wives as well. It was crucial that one of his wives give birth to a son who could take over as pharaoh someday.

Not all pharaohs were adults. Tutankhamen, or King Tut, became a pharaoh when he was around nine. And not all pharaohs were men, either. A woman might take over as pharaoh when there was no male heir. Some of these women ruled jointly, with a husband, brother, son, or other male relative.

Memorable Pharaohs

Hatshepsut: She reigned for more than a decade and had tremendous power for a woman. She was often depicted in statues and other artwork as a man.

Akhenaton: The husband of Nefertiti and possibly the father of Tutankhamen, he replaced all the old Egyptian deities with a sun god named Aton, whom he claimed was his "father." (When Tutankhamen assumed power, he brought back all the old gods.)

Tutankhamen: "King Tut" became pharaoh when he was around nine and died when he was around eighteen. In 1922, an archaeologist named Howard Carter discovered his tomb in the Valley of the Kings; it contained not only King Tut's mummy and the mummies of family members but an extraordinary treasure trove. Some consider this to be the most important archaeological find of the twentieth century.

Ramses II was the second-longest ruler in the history of Egypt. He had more than one hundred children.

PYRAMIDS

Ancient Egyptians built many pyramids throughout the kingdom. They were an extraordinary achievement in architecture.

Pyramids were tombs for the pharaohs, and a pharaoh was buried in his or her very own pyramid after he or she died.

Pharaohs weren't always buried in pyramids, though. The earliest kings were buried in rectangular buildings called mastabas. Then an architect named Imhotep decided to get fancy and came up with the idea of a "step pyramid." A step pyramid consisted of six rectangles stacked on top of each other, with each one getting smaller as it rose to the sky. The first one was created for a king named Djoser. The pharaohs after him created bigger and bigger pyramids.

The famous Great Pyramid of Giza was built for a pharaoh named Khufu. It took twenty years, more than two million stone blocks, and anywhere from twenty thousand to a hundred thousand men (depending on who you ask) to construct it. For nearly four thousand years, it was the tallest man-made structure in the world.

The Sphinx

The Great Sphinx of Giza, commonly known as "The Sphinx," is an enormous sculpture with the head of a human and the body of a lion. Many believe that it was built for Khufu's son Khafre, who was pharaoh around 2500 BCE. Khafre was responsible for the second, smaller pyramid at Giza. (Menkaure, Khafre's successor, was responsible for the third pyramid at Giza.)

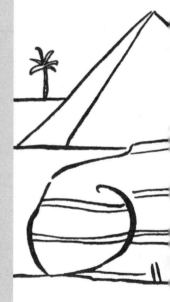

THE AFTERLIFE

When a person in Ancient Egypt died, he or she didn't really "die."

Ancient Egyptians believed in something called an afterlife, or life after death. This meant that a person could continue living even after he or she was technically dead.

To do this, the person's body was made into a mummy, or mummified, to keep from decaying. Certain organs, like the stomach and lungs, were removed and stored in special pots called canopic jars. The body was packed with a kind of salt and allowed to dry. After it

dried, the body was wrapped with strips of linen cloth. Amulets, or magic charms, might be placed among the wrappings. The mummy's face was covered with a decorative mask.

Finally, the mummy was put inside a case called a sarcophagus. The sarcophagus might have paintings on it to help the person make the journey to the next life. A funerary text called the 'Book of the Dead' contained magic spells and was also meant to help with the journey.

The sarcophagus was then buried in a tomb along with the canopic jars. The tomb would also contain things that the person might need in his or her afterlife. For ordinary citizens, this might be food, clothes, and cosmetics. The pharaohs, however, were often buried with tons of furniture, jewelry, artwork, and other valuable items. But over time, tomb robbers stole much of the treasure from these burial sites.

Pets and other animals were often mummified and buried with their owners so they could be together in the afterlife.

EVERYDAY LIFE

Now you know about the afterlife. But what was everyday life like in Ancient Egypt? What if you had actually lived there?

Let's pretend: You are a citizen of Ancient Egypt. Your father is a fisherman, and your mother takes care of you and your sisters and brothers at home.

Your have two pets, a dog and a baboon. You also have a cat, although cats in Ancient Egypt were considered to be magical guardians of the home rather than plain old ordinary pets.

Your family lives in a small, dimly lit house. There is almost no furniture, because wood is hard to come by. Statues of gods and goddesses line the walls; you pray to them to keep you healthy and safe. At night, you sleep on a brick platform.

Your daily outfit is a white kilt or tunic. You walk around in sandals or bare feet. You might have a shaved head. Some Egyptians shaved their hair to stay cool and avoid lice. Others wore wigs.

Everyone in your family wears eye makeup. Eyes are lined with black galena (later called kohl) and green malachite. These substances are ground up and mixed with animal fat. Eye makeup is believed to protect against evil, heal irritations, repel insects, block the sun's glare, and strengthen eyesight. Women also like to paint their lips and cheeks with ocher, an earthy red pigment found in nature, for decoration.

It hardly ever rains, so your family gets all the water it needs from the Nile River. You drink from the Nile, you bathe in the Nile, and you do your laundry in the Nile. And of course, your father catches all his fish in the Nile.

Your parents shop for food and other necessities at the market in your village. The market is right on the Nile so that ships and boats can deliver their cargo to the stalls easily. Goods can also be carried to the market by donkey.

The market is always bustling with activity. Craftspeople make baskets, sandals, jewelry, and furniture to sell. Farmers offer lettuce, melon, and other crops. Women bake bread out of wheat and barley. Children play with balls, spinning tops, and clay dolls. Cats, monkeys, and other animals wander around.

You ask your parents to buy some grapes, because they are your favorite! You also like figs, cucumbers, and bread with honey. Money has not been invented yet, so your parents trade; this is called bartering. Since your father is a fisherman, he would likely barter with his freshly caught perch, eels, or catfish.

Back home, most of the cooking is done outside.
Meat roasts on spits. Loaves of bread bake on the
outside of clay ovens and fall off when they are
done. Stews simmer in big pots that sit on top of
open fires. Fish fry in pans that sit on top of tripods.

For fun, you might play games or sports with your family and friends. Popular board games include *mehen*, also called the "game of the snake," and *senet*, which involves skill and chance. Kids also enjoy their own versions of tug-of-war, leapfrog, and hopscotch as well as racing and wrestling.

You don't go to school, although you do help your father with his fishing business. Other children might work for their parents or learn skills from them like weaving and taking care of farm animals.

Only children from wealthy families go to school, and most of them are boys. These children attend special schools to learn how to be scribes. Scribes read and write tax records, medical texts, and other important documents. Most Ancient Egyptians don't know how to read or write, so scribes are very valuable.

The language you and your family speak is called Egyptian. If you could read and write, you would use hieroglyphics, which are pictures that represent words, syllables, or sounds. Hieroglyphics are written on stone slates, pottery fragments, or papyrus. In modern Egypt the main language is Arabic.

If you are a boy, you might become a fisherman, a farmer, a builder, or a craftsperson when you grow up. If you are a girl, you might become a baker or a dancer or a musician; you might also get married at a young age, like fourteen. Your friends who went to school might become scribes, priests, lawyers, or doctors.

Population

At one time, ancient Egypt had a population of about three million people. Today, Egypt has a population of about eighty-two million. That's a big difference!

HEALTH AND MEDICINE

Oh no, you have a stomachache! Maybe you ate too many grapes and figs at the market.

Lucky for you, there are many doctors in Ancient Egypt!

A doctor back then might be a scribe or priest who received formal medical training—or not. The so-called Houses of Life within temples stored medical texts and sometimes offered instruction, too. A person might also gain medical training by apprenticing for an older relative who happened to be a doctor.

Doctors could recognize and treat hundreds of illnesses. Common ailments in Ancient Egypt included dental disease, scorpion and snakebites, and eye problems due to all the sand blowing around and getting into people's eyes.

Doctors were good at talking to their patients and observing their symptoms. They understood the connection between a person's pulse and heart. They knew how to fix broken bones, perform surgeries, and make medicines. These medicines often contained garlic, onion, or herbs like cumin, coriander, or mint.

Doctors also used spells, amulets, and other magical practices to make their patients healthy. Ancient Egyptians believed that an evil spirit in the body could cause sickness. Spells were thought to drive out such spirits. So were gross things like crocodile poop! Other healing ingredients included pigs' teeth for upset stomachs, hedgehog quills for baldness, and milk from a woman who had given birth to a boy, for colds.

Is your stomachache better? Or would you like some pigs' teeth?

CRIME AND PUNISHMENT

What happened if you broke a law in Ancient Egypt?

Ancient Egyptians had a legal system in place to deal with criminals. A legal system provides rules for people to follow and punishments for the rulebreakers. In Ancient Egypt, the legal system was based on the principal of *maat*. (You'll remember that *maat* has to do with order, harmony, truth, and justice.)

Thieves were punished, and so were people who didn't show up for their jobs, deserted the army, or committed other crimes. Stealing from a tomb was considered to be one of the worst crimes of all, because it meant taking away a dead person's ability to find his or her way to the afterlife.

The pharaoh was in charge of Egypt's legal system, which included police officers, government officials, and judges. The rulebreakers were usually put on trial. If found guilty, the criminal might be sentenced to jail, hard labor, or exile, which meant he or she had to leave home and live in some faraway, not-very-nice place. There were more severe punishments as well that involved physical pain or even death.

Sometimes, the criminal's family was considered guilty of the crime, too. For example, if a man was sentenced to exile, his wife and children might also be exiled.

THE END OF
A CIVILIZATION

Ancient Egypt had periods of war and periods
of peace. The pharaoh had soldiers to defend the
kingdom from invaders and conquer new lands.

ROME MACEDONIA

mediterranean Sea

Alexandria Buto

Pelusium

PERSIA

NILE

ESNA

In the last thousand years BCE, Egypt was invaded and conquered by one nation after another, including Persia, Macedonia, and Rome. Egypt gradually lost its independence, which meant that it could no longer rule itself but had to be ruled by its conquerors.

Some of the conquerors respected Egyptian traditions, like Alexander the Great of Macedonia. Alexander was the king of Egypt for almost a decade.

After Alexander came his general Ptolemy, then a line of Ptolemy's heirs. Cleopatra the Seventh was the last in the Ptolemaic dynasty of pharaohs.

Ptolemy I

Cleopatra

Hellenic Ptolemy

Ptolemy VIII

Ptolemy XII

When the Romans invaded Egypt in 30 BCE, Egypt became part of the Roman Empire.

HOW DO WE KNOW ALL THIS?

How do we know what happened way back then?

This is where historians, archaeologists, and Egyptologists come in.

Over the years, archaeologists have dug up many objects from Ancient Egypt, like tools, weapons, pottery, musical instruments, jewelry, and paintings. These objects provide clues to what life in Ancient Egypt may have been like. So do the pyramids, temples, and other structures that are still standing in Egypt.

Mummies also provide important clues about that time, and offer information about the person who died. Take a mummy of a woman, for example. With X-rays, miniature cameras, modeling, and more, scientists can tell how old she was when she died, the state of her health, and even what kind of job she may have had.

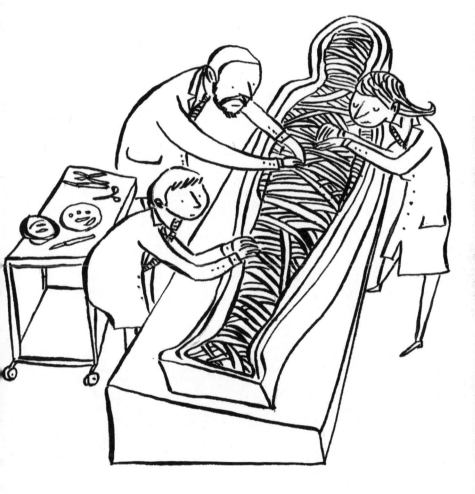

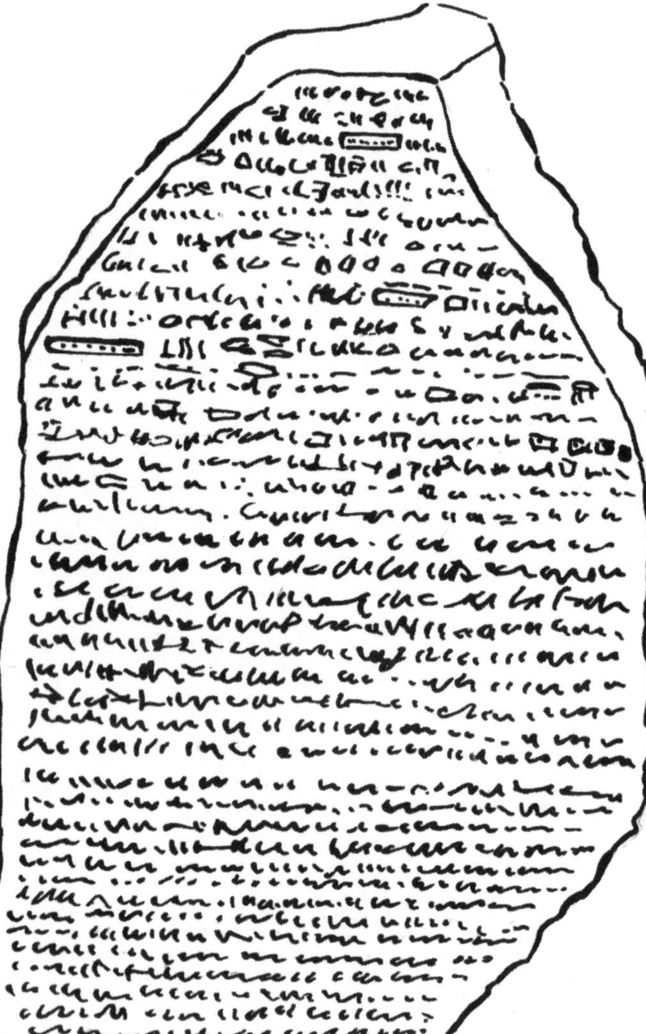

The Ancient Egyptians also left many written documents—except that they were in hieroglyphics. For a long time, no one understood what those hieroglyphics meant.

But the discovery of the Rosetta stone in 1799 changed all that. This stone tablet had the same words carved into it in three different kinds of writing: Ancient Greek, hieroglyphics, and demotic script, which was a type of cursive writing. By comparing all three versions of the text, scholars were finally able to understand hieroglyphics!

Still, experts can and do disagree about what documents and other archaeological remains mean. Different scholars have different theories about what happened, how it happened, when it happened, and so forth. The record is incomplete.

Maybe you'll figure out a piece of the puzzle of Ancient Egypt someday!

THE LEGACY OF ANCIENT EGYPT

A legacy is something given from the past to the present.

The Ancient Egyptian civilization gave us art, jewelry, pottery, statues, and other beautiful objects.

It gave us glorious architecture that still influences how buildings are built today.

Ancient Egyptian creations and inspirations are still with us. Some historians believe that toothpaste, breath mints, eye makeup, devices that tell time, the plow, the door lock, and bowling can all be traced back to Ancient Egypt. And even though the Chinese are credited with the invention of paper (in approximately 105 CE), the Egyptians used the papyrus plant to make the other kind of papyrus, the paper-like writing material, thousands of years before that.

Thank you, Ancient Egypt!

Well, it's been a great adventure. Good-bye, Ancient Egypt!

Where to next?

Coming in July 2016!

Selected Bibliography

Ancient Egypt by Philip Ardagh, Peter Bedrick Books, 2000

Ancient Egypt by George Hart, Dorling Kindersley, Inc., 1990

Ancient Egypt by Lorna Oakes and Lucia Gahlin,
    Hermes House, 2004

Ancient Egypt Revealed by Peter Chrisp, DK Publishing, 2002

Ancient Egyptian Jobs by John Malam, Heinemann Library, 2003

Egyptian Life by John Guy, Barron's Educational Series, Inc., 1998

Egyptian Mythology by Simon Goodenough, Todtri
    Productions Ltd., 1997

Encyclopedia Brittanica Online, www.brittanica.com

Everything Ancient Egypt by Crispin Boyer with James P. Allen,
    President of the International Association of Egyptologists,
    National Geographic Society, 2012

The House of Life: Per Ankh; Magic and Medical Science in Ancient Egypt
    by Paul Ghalioungui, B. M. Israel, 1963

Treasury of Egyptian Mythology by Donna Jo Napoli, National
    Geographic Society, 2013

NANCY OHLIN is the author of the YA novels *Always, Forever* and *Beauty* as well as the early chapter book series Greetings from Somewhere under the pseudonym Harper Paris. She lives in Ithaca, New York, with her husband, their two kids, two cats, a bunny, and assorted animals who happen to show up at their door. Visit her online at nancyohlin.com.

ADAM LARKUM is a freelance illustrator based in the United Kingdom. In his fifteen years of illustrating, he's worked on over forty books. In addition to his illustration work, he also dabbles in animation and develops characters for television.

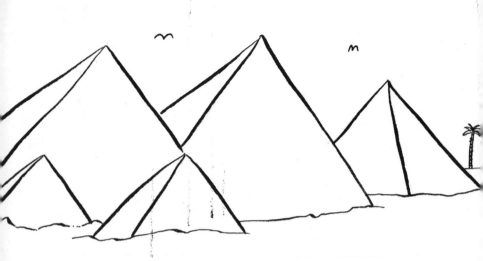